41 Ways to Get Money For Your Business

Proven Strategies

Your Pathway To Business Funding

By: Gil Zapata a.k.a. "Mr. Gil"
CEO & Founder of
Lendinero.com

LENDINERO

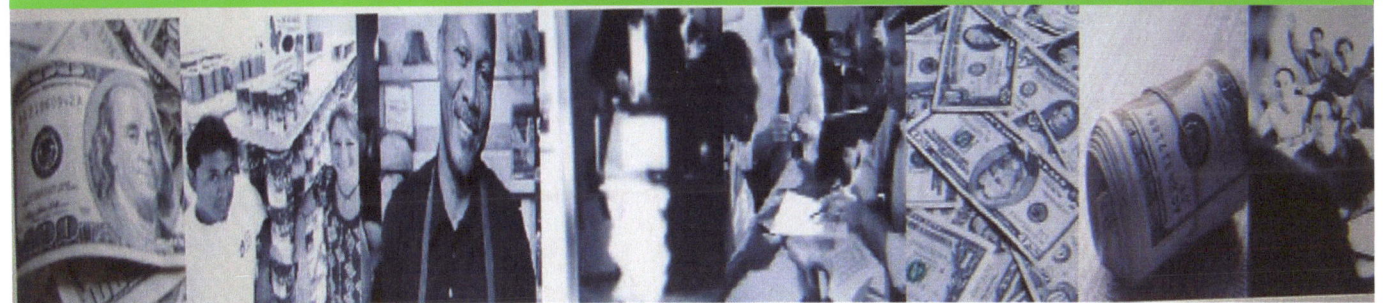

Copyright © 2011 Gil Zapata
Sponsored by: Lendinero.com

All rights reserved.

ISBN: 1477515704
ISBN-13: 9781477515709

DEDICATION

This Book is dedicated to all the entrepreneurs and business owners out there who are seeking to live their dream. As the author of this book I know what it's like to lack capital when starting a business and growing a business. Don't let capital be an obstacle in starting or growing your business venture. In today's day and age you have to be creative and innovative. Some of my clients, friends, partners, and me have utilized some of these methods.

If you implement at least one idea that will help you access even just the minimal amount of capital for your business we want you to share your success stories. We can only succeed if you succeed. This country, this world needs more people like you. It's better to invent a job than to find one. You are inventing your own job and jobs for others. This is what we need to turn around the world economy.

Disclaimer & Legal stuff

Copyright 2012 Gil Zapata ©. All Rights Reserved.

Please feel free to share this document freely but please do not modify out of professional courtesy. This report is based on the author's personal experiences regarding business funding. Also, this book is not available for re-sale without consent of the author. If you would like to distribute this publication via your blog, on-line store, book store, or if you are publisher please contact us. We will be more than happy to share revenues with you.

There are no guarantees concerning the level of success you might experience with this report. We make every effort to ensure accuracy of information, but there are no guarantees that your results will match the examples published in this report.

Some information, technology and links may change for reasons beyond the control of the author and/ or affiliates.

contact@lendinero.com
www.lendinero.com
www.twitter.com/lendinero
www.facebook.com/lendinero

About the Author

Gil Zapata, aka "MR.GIL", is the founder of Lendinero.com a, KGFA Capital Ventures LLC company. The company originally founded in 2003 as KGFA Capital Partners LLC was an originator of commercial real estate finance, dealer financing for businesses and alternative investments. Today, Gil continues to lead the firm's development as KGFA Capital Ventures, a company specializing in helping businesses and entrepreneurs obtain business funding through alternative channels.

Mr. Zapata also works as a Senior Business Advisor for CEO Advisors, a Multi National Strategic Business Advisement Firm, providing business owners consulting services on strategy, internet technology, innovative marketing, strategic financing, structured financing, venture capital, joint ventures, mergers and acquisitions, and other solutions.

Gil has been involved in highly complex financing transactions for over 15 years. His involvement in these transactions has been in the capacity of a broker, placement agent, equity investor, and advisor. Today, Gil's expertise has grown to include:

- Private Placements / Alternative Investments
- Mutual Fund Placements / Asset Allocation
- Private Equity Transactions & Venture Capital
- Factoring / Purchase Order Financing
- Dealer Financing / Consumer Financing
- Cross Collateral & Debt to Equity Swaps
- Leverage Buy Outs / Sell Side Advisory / Buy Side Advisory
- Joint Ventures and Limited Partnerships
- Sales & Marketing Integration with Financing
- Public Equities
- Secondary Market Transactions
- Research & Development on Private & Public Financing
- Non-Profit & Public Financing
- Small Business Loans

Gil has counseled and advised consumers, small business owners, CEOs, Governing Board Members, entrepreneurs, individual investors, and investor groups not only in the United States, but in Cyprus (Europe), Central America, South America, and the Caribbean. Mr. Zapata has completed numerous financial transactions in a wide range of industries like business services, financial services, public equities, real estate, consumer services, distribution, manufacturing, print/ on-line media, non-profit organizations and internet technology. He has traveled the world and has business contacts in nearly every continent.

Gil has also participated in numerous Governing Boards and has been a founding member of several boards to include the Master's of Finance Advisory Board at Chapman Graduate

Business School at Florida International University, the New World Symphony, The Multicultural Project of the Americas, and other organizations. While in college, he completed an internship at the Florida Department of Commerce under then Governor Jeb Bush.

Gil has written and has been featured in numerous Publications and Television outlets.

Mr. Zapata began his career in Financial Services in 1994 working on a special financing and marketing project in his native country of Nicaragua. At that time, he coordinated the efforts of numerous multinational financial organizations and educational institutions.

Thereafter, he jointed John Hancock Financial Services where he obtained numerous licenses to include a Series 6 with the National Association of Securities Dealers. In 1998, he joined Bankers Securities Corp., a private finance boutique firm on Miami's prestigious Brickell Avenue. Here, he became Executive Vice-President of the firm. He directed the firm's retail real estate sales team and the secondary market trading division. In 2003 to pursue his entrepreneurial dreams, he initiated his own company, KGFA Capital Partners LLC. In 2011 with KGFA Capital becoming a branded financial enterprise, he transformed the company into a leading Funding Advisor to small and mid-sized businesses all over the U.S. Today, KGFA Capital is doing business as "lendinero.com" a nationwide on-line company specializing in alternative business funding providing multiple funding solutions to businesses.

Gil earned his B.A. degree from Florida International University in Miami FL., with the majority of coursework completed at Florida State University in Tallahassee, FL. Subsequently, he continued post-graduate studies at Florida International University in Public Administration and in Management & Executive Education at The Harvard Business School.

Gil has obtained numerous licenses in the Financial Services industry from The Florida Department of Financial Services and other National Regulatory Agencies. In addition, he has participated in highly sophisticated seminars and courses on private equity, venture capital, investment banking, and commercial lending from various private educational institutions.

Gil is fluent in English and Spanish and comprehends Italian, French, and Portuguese.

Gil resides in Miami, FL for the majority of the time. Currently, he conducts business in numerous parts of the world and is willing to follow an opportunity no matter where it leads.

Gil states, "If it takes 1 hour or 24 hours, 1 year or 10 years don't ever stop trying to achieve your goals and objectives even when obstacles and challenges arise. If it was that easy, everyone would do it. Successful people are willing to do and handle what unsuccessful people are not willing to. Success comes at a high price and sometimes may involve a high degree of risk, sacrifice, and uncomfortable junctures. Engage in the necessary activities to obtain the results you seek with adequate measure, patience, balance, perseverance, realistic time frames, resistance, ethical standards and other elements. The seeds you plant today will eventually become the crop you harvest tomorrow. Most people are looking for the lottery ticket which, in reality, does not exist. Personally, it is the little things you do today that will become the big things of tomorrow. There is no quick fix solution. It all takes time. If you are willing to withstand the test of time you will make it. Most people are used to instant gratification. The odds are 30 to 1.   30 People will try to shatter your dreams, tare you apart, and bring you down. So, always stay on course and keep going no matter how difficult it gets. There were over 1000 people or more along the way who were not in my favor. But, if I would have listened to just one of them, or let them get in my way, or try to destroy me, I would have never achieved anything. I still have a long way to go. I'm not even close to achieving 80% of the things I would like to do for others at a personal, business, community, and political level. Listen to yourself. Believe in yourself. Give it time and you can achieve just about anything. In the end, I also believe that success will not matter unless you give back. Leave a legacy. Always know what you want and your reason for being. What good is $10 Million after history has erased me from existence. How much do I really need if I started with $0 Capital? Thus, I would rather give back $5 Million and be remembered for changing lives and helping businesses and know that my contributions will live well beyond my existence. Have fun and enjoy the ride: the ups, the downs, and always the turns. Sometimes you win and sometimes you lose. People don't like to talk about failures. Thomas J. Watson, who built IMB once said, "If You Want To Succeed Double Your Rate of Failure". These are my words of wisdom and guidance.

Why Am I Doing This?
This is a very important question that I ask many entrepreneurs and business owners. Why are you doing this? As part of my business model, I come in contact with business owners every day. This daily contact has allowed me to learn, not only from my experiences, but from the experiences of other entrepreneurs and business owners. I have seen success and failure at their extremes. And while many people don't like to talk about failures, I know that it is one of the most important factors to any business or entrepreneur. Failure is one of the keys to success. There is no business school that can teach you what you will experience as an entrepreneur. I completed executive education at The Harvard Business School and was part of the board at The Chapman Graduate Business School at Florida International University. I have realized that Theory and Practice are two different things.

Over the past decade, the Team at KGFA Capital has not only studied the great entrepreneurs of history, but also had real-time experiences working with and guiding thousands of successful entrepreneurs.   Most of our team members have also been entrepreneurs in an individual capacity as well.

So, I know what it's like to be at the top of the business chain, the bottom, the challenges, the rewards, etc. I just wish that I had had the proper mentorship in my past. I learned the hard way through the school of trial and error. My mission to help out as many other entrepreneurs and business owners as possible was born out my experiences and hardships. For those that are starting out, I know that money and funding can be one major hurdle. At KGFA Capital, I have numerous services to help out business owners. Lendinero.com is our focus. We are implementing the latest technology that will allow businesses to obtain multiple funding approvals to reach their capital needs in the business life cycle. Soon, we will create a charitable Foundation to help out business owners and entrepreneurs who cannot afford the high cost of business consulting, strategic management, and acquiring funding. My goal is to help out as many businesses as possible, leaving a legacy of a contributor to the betterment of our economy, society, and families.

To Your Success!
Gil Zapata "Mr. Gil"
Founder & CEO "LENDINERO.COM"
A KGFA Capital Ventures LLC Co.

"IT ALL STARTS WITH A DREAM, DREAM BIG"

Most entrepreneurs and business owners feel that the only way to obtain funding is by getting a business loan. However, this is a big Myth as most successful companies utilize innovative ways to get funding periodically. Today, more than ever, there are unlimited channels that one can tap into to obtain alternative funding." Below, is a list that I find crucial for every business owner and entrepreneur to explore:

1. Bootstrap .

I placed this one at the top of the list for one reason: Bootstrap your way to success . Re invest all or most of the profits of your business right back into to it until it becomes self-sustaining. Bootstrapping is also about finding a way to sell your products or your services. Most aspiring entrepreneurs or newly formed businesses credit money as the biggest obstacle for not starting or expanding their business. However, the fact of the matter is that the most important factor in a business is Sales and Revenue. Nothing happens without a sale. If you cannot sell your product or services, there will be no revenues. So, if you can sell and generate revenues, obtaining funding becomes much easier. Some businesses may not be able to sell right away because they need technology or to manufacture a product. In this is the case, find a product or service or a company that has a similar product or service and begin selling it as an agent or broker.

2. Fundraising From Individual People.

This may sound crazy, but it works. You can do this on-line or you can do it face to face. First come up with a list of at least 200 people. If you don't know 200 people; start with 10 and then ask them to list other people or go out and meet people. You can join a club, association, church group, or any other organization that has access to a lot of people. Keep in mind that every business is about people and if you are not a people person then you need to get someone on your team who is a people person. Business in the end boils down to people; investors, consumers, clients, bankers, attorneys, accountants, and other people who you will need to come across with at one point in time. Emails and text are useful, but the voice contact and face to face contact method is probably the most effective way to communicate because you can express your enthusiasm, body language, and other cues which an email or a text cannot. Once you have the list compiled, let them know what you are doing and ask them to donate or invest a small amount of money anywhere from $50 to $200. Now imagine if 100 people donated $150 each to you, you would raise $15,000. If you have a clientele base, this becomes even easier because you can offer incentives, special discounts, and packages if people pre-pay, donate, or invest.

3. Personal Savings .

There's nothing like having your own money saved to invest into your startup. You have the satisfaction of having saved it on your own, and the knowledge that you don't owe anyone.
Risk: It's your money, and if you're not successful, the money is gone, and with it the opportunity to do anything else with it later.

4. Partner Savings .

Having a partner helps spread out not only the business management but the financial burden. A good partnership is also synergetic, bringing more success than running a business alone. Find a partner who has better credit than you or who may have savings. You may need to give them 10%, 30% or 50% of some of your earnings depending on how you structure the partnership with them. However, if you are going to bring in a partner who has savings or who is willing to put up their personal credit for you, make sure that you don't give them a large percentage of earnings unless they can generate revenues or add value. Otherwise, just offer them a fixed rate of return. The last thing you want is a partner who put up capital but adds no value or cannot help generate revenues for the prosperity of the company.

Risk : A fed up partner who wants out; arguments; irresponsible partners who leave you with all the debt; broken friendships.

5. Contact Partner.

Contacts or the right contacts can make a big difference in business. You can find a partner, consultant, or someone who has the right contacts. This means contacts with money and capital to invest, who can lead to joint ventures, who can direct you in the right direction, who can introduce you to important decision makers, etc. This is very valuable. This is a hidden treasure. If you have a contact partner or consultant who knows 10 people who have over $1 Million in the bank, you have access to over $10 Million. If you have a partner, for example, who may help you form a joint venture with a bigger company that may utilize your services or products, this may lead to immediate revenues and cash. Someone who is very well connected can make a huge difference in the world of business. Imagine, if you know someone that can sit you in front of Warren Buffet, Carlos Slim, or Donald Trump even for a minute.

6. Sell your Stuff.

Sell anything you haven't used in a year or longer. The same goes for leased items. Dig around your house and find things to sell which you don't really need. If you don't have any items to sell, place an ad saying "I will take your unwanted items" or "Unwanted Furniture I will Collect It", or any ad along those same lines. Place those items for sale on craigslist.com. This may even become a side business with time. However, don't lose track of what you ultimately want to do.

Risk : Regrets, or worse: going out and spending to replace the item(s) you sold.

7. Windfalls.

Invest tax refunds, gifts, lottery winnings into your business. If you don't have the money to invest your tax refunds or gifts, buy 2 lottery tickets or scratch offs per day. You can buy lottery tickets with prizes of $1 Million or more. Personally, I would buy the ones that payout $5,000, $10,000 or $50,000. The chances of winning smaller amounts of money are greater.

Risk : Getting hooked on lotteries and gambling to "fund" your dream business.

8. Barter and resell.

Consider offering products or services that you can barter in return for something that you can sell for a profit. A very extreme execution of the bartering principle is Kyle MacDonald's One Red Paperclip experiment. He started with a red paper clip, and through a series of swap/barter transactions, he ended up with a house within a year, and is now trying to trade it, potentially for cash. Barter your services. If you need office space, a car, or something else and you have a service or product you can offer the other person then make the deal. I have applied this tactic in numerous ways. One time, I offered students to help them get scholarships in exchange to work for me at no cost to me. You need to be creative.

9. Retirement savings plan.

Dip into your retirement savings, especially if there's a government incentive (i.e., qualified tax break). Sometimes, retirement accounts let you borrow against them. Even if you have to pay an early withdrawal penalty of 10% or even 20%, if you are a true business owner don't look at the loss, determine your return on investment. If you take out $50,000 and you have pay 10% which is $5,000, you only have $45,000. But, the magical question is Can you double that money within 1 year in your business? Or, can this money help you sustain and make some investments into your business during the next several months to start generating cash flow or increase earnings.

10. Credit cards.

It might be easier to use your lines of credit (which you'll have if you have a good credit score). However, personal or business lines of credit are almost impossible to obtain today. So, if you have existing credit cards, simply use them. If you don't have any or have bad credit find a credit partner.

11. Credit card arbitrage.

This is an extension of the credit card approach, and uses the "0% balance transfer " options that were so common a few years ago. Today, there are still credit cards with 0% interest introductory rates.

12. Borrow money.

Borrow from family, friends, colleagues, or employees, etc. An alternative to this is to have one of the aforementioned co-sign a bank loan for you.

13. Get a bank loan.

If you have a solid business plan and a decent credit score then the lender may agree to give you a loan. This can often be the least expensive (interest rate-wise) loan source available. Today, however, most banks require a personal guarantee. And, if your credit score or cash flow is not strong, it will be difficult to obtain a loan from a bank.

14. Home equity.

If you have equity in your real estate holdings, some lenders will accept that as collateral for a business loan. Alternately, you could refinance your home, taking a mortgage with a lower monthly payment to free up some funds for business. With the Real Estate downfall, of course, this is becoming much more difficult to obtain. However, you may need to find property owners who paid cash and that have 100% equity. You need to learn how to structure these deals financially and how to utilize numerous mechanisms and financing structures to assure payment, collateral, and other factors.

15. Cash out your life insurance policy.

This has been a common way for entrepreneurs to fund their startups. If you have an insurance policy see how much money you have accumulated.

16. Grants.

There are often a variety of government grant programs for specific types of startup businesses. You can search online. I would also go and visit or call your local city, state officials to inquire about possible funding sources.

17. Donations via social media.

For example, the Tweets Giving Drive via Twitter pulled in over $10,000 in just 48 hours from individual donations of just $5 or $10 dollars. This sort of approach works thanks to online payment processing services such as PayPal . Build up your followers on your Facebook's friends list. You will need about 200 people or more. Also, you need to build a campaign. It is not just about placing a donation page or a link. You will need to send messages, emails, place postings and working your account.

18. Crowd Funding Sites.

There are sites where you can post your funding request for your business or product. However, there are many hidden tactics that you will need to learn. I have seen businesses get $1,000 up to $1 Million on these sites within a 120 day time frame. It's not just posting a video and asking for money. There are strategies and tactics that can make you or break you.

19. Micro loans.

Accion USA, Kiva , Prosper , etc. These may be relatively small, but if combined with a scale up sales strategy you may be able to get some sort of funding. In some cases, Prosper requires a 640 to 660 credit score. But, some micro lenders may accept a credit score as low as 580.

20. Startup incubator.

Business incubators such as YCombinator exist in various industries, but are more likely to fund tech niches than anything else. They tend to be more accepting of promising ideas and smart entrepreneurs. This type of funding is sometimes known as "seed financing."

21. Investor capital.

Get angel investments or venture capital. Convert blood money lenders into investors or silent partners. Or find many angel investors, as they tend to give smaller loans than VCs (Venture Capitalists). Venture capital is not a common option for most startups, but might come an excellent source at a later stage of your business. Note, that at a later stage, your customers and suppliers could very well be investors. There are a number of Venture Capital firms that provide seed capital. You need to know which ones they are. Sometimes, these Venture Capital firms can provide $50,000 to $500,000 in start up funds. However, most of the Venture Capital firms like tech companies, innovative products, and other specific type companies.

22. Leasing Real Estate.

You don't need to be a realtor to do lease options. This is a business within a business. You need to find landlords or properties and place an option for lease and tell the landlord that you are willing to lease the property for a longer period of time, such as 2 years. You agree on a discounted price and then you lease it at the market price and the difference is residual income for you. However, your spread may be very little. For instance, you may just make $100 to $200 per month on properties that are very marketable. However, if you had 10 properties you are doing this with, you could be making a residual income that could cover any losses.

23. Factoring companies.

Factoring companies buy your pending invoices (accounts receivable) and give you cash, minus a transaction fee.

24. Online Retail Financing.

If you operate an online retail business, there is no need to go out and purchase inventory. Today, I know of a lender who will finance the inventory for online retailers at 7% to 10% interest rate.

25. Check re-discounting.

This is similar to factoring. However, check re-discounters take a postdated check you have written today to advance you the funds, minus a fee.

26. Private offering.

Turn your blood money lenders into part owners, so that they have an emotionally vested stake in seeing your business succeed. This is also known as a private placement. Private Placements are usually exempt from the Securities and Exchange Commission. You do need to know what documents you will need, like Private Placement Memorandums, Subscription Documents, Promissory Notes, Convertible Promissory Notes, Debentures, etc. The deal type will determine documents needed.

27. Public offering.

A public offering widens your potential for selling shares and thus getting operating capital when you need it. A public offering does not mean that you have to register your company with the New York Stock Exchange. But, you have to be very careful in the manner that you do it. I would consult an attorney first.

28. Consignment.

This isn't so much a fund source as it is a source of products to earn revenue and to pay "suppliers" after their products have been sold. Small boutique shops often take this approach, thereby reducing their operating costs to rent, electricity, phone and a few other items. Inventory costs drop potentially to nothing.

29. Coupon Sites.

Depending on the business you have, not all businesses are fit for coupon sites. If you don't have a service or product you can offer, you need to find a way to make this happen. This can be a fast way to bring in revenues. However, you will have to conduct a price analysis if you do not want to end up working for FREE or be at a loss. But, coupon sites allow you to obtain pre-paid customers very quickly. I have done this before for other businesses and we have seen 100 to 300 sales in 1 day. Furthermore, from a price analysis point, you need to conduct a service time analysis, a delivery of service analysis, and other things to assure that you can fulfill the amount of sales completed. Also, this allows for your business to be branded on-line at no additional costs and, depending on the product or service, you may be able to up sell, cross sell, or find new sale opportunities to customers you never had before.

30. Employer intrapreneurship programs.

Companies sometimes have programs that allow qualified employees time, resources and even funding to explore business ideas or new technology.

31. Entrepreneurship programs.

This is similar to intrapreneurship programs but is not limited to employees of a company or organization.

32. Online ad revenue.

This is an option that has only become available in the last few years. If you have the skills to build, promote and monetize a web site - which you can be started for practically nothing - then you might profit either by selling it or using advertising or other revenue (premium content sales, subscription fees, consulting, etc.) to fund your startup.

33. Freelancing or contracting .

You may not be able to hold down a regular job while also running a startup; but, part-time freelancing or contract work might be an option for generating extra income. Sometimes, you may be able to find freelance jobs that are aligned with your business agenda. If you are seriously considering building your business or a business, freelance work is better than a full time job. The success rate of most people who have a full-time job and are launching or want to launch a business is close zero. (see: guru.com)

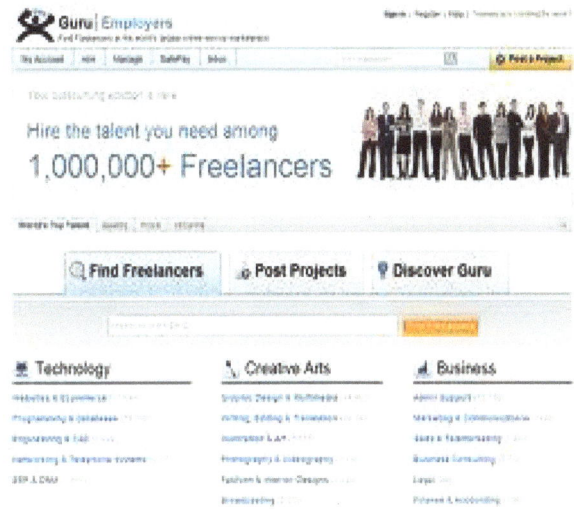

34. Auctioning your name.

If you don't like your personal name or are otherwise willing to change it to a company or brand name, you might be able cash in for many thousands of dollars.

35. Domain Auctioning.

This is almost the same thing as number 34. If you own a domain or can buy a catchy name domain, you buy it and then you place it up for sale.

36. Selling Ad Space.

Sell advertising space on your body. Options include wearing signboards, t-shirts with company logos, or temporary or permanent tattoos. A less drastic option is to sell ad space on your car. You can sell ad space on your web site if you have a lot of traffic.

37. Awards/ competitions.

Universities and companies occasionally have business/ entrepreneurial competitions.

38. Dividends.

If you have mutual funds or stocks in your investment portfolio that pay out regular dividends, this could be a potential source of startup funds. This way, you do not have to cash in your portfolio's principal investment, so it can continue to earn for you.

39. Real estate.

Sure, the market is not the best right now. But, there are a lot of cash buyers out there. You may not have the credit or the money to buy real estate, but you can place option contracts and then sell the contract at a premium.

40. Broadcast & Network.

The most important thing is to broadcast about yourself and let yourself be known. Most small business owners have some fear of people or fear that someone is going to copy their ideas. If you were Microsoft, Dell, or any other well known company, you would notice that anyone can also take their products and make them better or different. Don't fear anyone copying your idea. This is the world of capitalism and competition. There is certain information you should disclose and other which you should never leak. You should know what is proprietary and valuable to you.

41. Find the Right People

Most people make the mistake of knocking on the wrong door. I will give you an example; I am in the process of raising $1 Million for my company, which integrates technology. We want to be the leading Hispanic micro business lending portal. I started researching Hispanic entrepreneurs who are in the tech business, who have been successful in similar ventures, or have worked at venture capital firms. I am looking for a connection. On that note, I won't go and talk to a restaurant owner to fund the expansion of my business. If you are looking to play baseball you need to talk to baseball players. You get the idea?

I hope you have enjoyed this. If just one idea works for you please let me know. I am looking for entrepreneurs and small business owners to feature on my upcoming Video Series. Also, your feedback is very important. Write to me or to our company at:

contact@lendinero.com
www.lendinero.com
www.facebook.com/lendinero
www.twitter.com/lendinero

www.ingramcontent.com/pod-product-compliance
Lightning Source LLC
Chambersburg PA
CBHW041309180526
45172CB00003B/1036